Barbara Hepworth *Single Form* (*Memorial*) 1962
(bronze, 123″ H)
Battersea Park, London

Designed by Gillian Greenwood

Alan Bowness

MODERN SCULPTURE

studio vista | dutton pictureback

General editor David Herbert

Jacques Lipchitz *Man Leaning on his Elbow* 1925
(bronze, 5″ H)
Courtesy of Marlborough-Gerson Gallery, New York

© Alan Bowness 1965
Published in Great Britain by Studio Vista Limited
Blue Star House, Highgate Hill, London N19
and in the United States of America, by E. P. Dutton and Co Inc
201 Park Avenue South, New York, NY 10003
Reprinted 1966. 1967, 1969
Set in 8 pt Univers 2 pt leaded
Made and printed in Great Britain by
Richard Clay (The Chaucer Press), Ltd, Bungay, Suffolk

SBN 289 36807 3 (paperback)

CONTENTS

Introduction

This is not a history of modern sculpture but an essay about it. I have chosen four key ideas—the image of man, pure form and expressive surface, the role of magic and metamorphosis, the use of new materials—and have discussed them in a loose historical framework. These ideas are illustrated by the works which seem particularly relevant. No attempt has been made to present a comprehensive selection of modern sculpture in the plates of this volume, nor is the text a survey of the whole field. There are several excellent books which provide this, and they are listed in the bibliography on page 157.

I have tried instead to discuss some of the problems that have preoccupied sculptors in the last hundred years. Artists are men with problems—they return again and again, propounding a fresh solution, but the solution only raises as many questions as it answers. So it is that for the artist painting leads on to painting, sculpture to sculpture. Outside considerations, of course, affect this progression, but much less than the general public imagines. Equally, the wider relevance of what he is doing often escapes the artist, as does its relative significance. In a sense this is not his concern. He puts the work in the world, and what the world makes of it is, in the last resort, beyond his control.

Most of the discussion in the pages that follow centres around the work of sculptors active in the first half of this century. These are the heroic years of modern sculpture, when, following Rodin's great example, the art was reborn. I have not written about more recent developments, except in passing, because the picture is inevitably much less clear, and this would, in any case, require a book in itself. But, as with so much contemporary art, our appreciation is enhanced when we understand what precedes the present. It is for those who are puzzled by modern sculpture, and would like to know a little of what it is all about that this essay has been written.

Alberto Giacometti *Project for a Monument to a Celebrated Person* 1956 (plaster, 18″ H)
Private Collection, USA

Edgar Degas *Dancer Looking at the Sole of her Right Foot c.* 1911
(bronze, 18⅝" H)
Courtesy of The Trustees of The Tate Gallery, London

1 Images of man

The history of sculpture is dominated by images of ourselves. No other art is homocentric to a comparable degree, and this has been both the greatness and the limitation of sculpture. These images of man can relate directly to our bodily feelings, so that we find ourselves totally involved, emotionally and physically as well as intellectually, while we contemplate them. Yet only the greatest of artists achieve this, and great sculptors are much rarer than great painters or poets. Great sculptors have successfully triumphed over the restricted subject matter that has seemed to be all that was allowed them, but lesser sculptors have found the constant repetition of a narrow range of figures in varying poses a severe limitation.

It is a limitation that at various times in history has all but crippled the sculptor's creative imagination and reduced the art to being the scarcely regarded servant of architecture. Commissioned funerary monuments have provided the sculptor with his only opportunities of doing something more than providing decoration for buildings. Such monuments may be magnificent in themselves, but with rare exceptions they are the work of master craftsmen rather than of artists.

In ages of Humanism when man is regarded with greater veneration, and God, personified by His houses—the cathedrals and churches—seems less all-powerful, the sculptor comes into his own. He is known by name—Phidias or Michelangelo—and acclaimed for his life-size figures of man and woman. These are ideal images of ourselves, expressive of our aspirations. They have a timeless, universal validity, but they can only be made at moments of complete confidence.

Throughout the nineteenth century the prestige of antique and Renaissance sculpture was unchallenged. The general atmosphere was a humanist one, in which the possibilities before man seemed endless and in every way rewarding; and yet (as often happens when material values predominate) the general aesthetic was not an idealist but a naturalist one, just as it had been in Republican Rome. The attempt at the end of the eighteenth century to make a new ideal image of man, valid for the times, had failed: Canova the exponent of neo-classicism, was no Phidias or Michelangelo, and the outstanding sculptor of the day, Houdon, excelled only in portraiture.

The problem for the nineteenth-century sculptor was that naturalism is a much less viable artistic aim for a sculptor than it is, say, for a painter or novelist. Remarkable though a roomful of Roman portrait busts are, they leave us unmoved in comparison with a single and mutilated piece of fine Greek statuary. It is an undisputed fact that the best nineteenth-century sculpture was done not by the professionals but by amateurs—by painters, who turned to sculpture and made a few pieces, or tackled a limited problem—Géricault, Daumier, Degas, Gauguin, and the line of succession continues until today, as we shall see. These men were greater *artists* than the full-time sculptors: had they been born half a century later, they might well have spent more time making sculpture. Indeed, I think the true talents of certain of them—Daumier, for example—lay in three-dimensional visual art, but conditions, social and artistic, were so discouraging as to make a sculptor's career impossible.

The naturalistic aesthetic that was dominant until the 1880s demanded maximum verisimilitude. In painting this produced the Realism of Courbet and then, when the unifying power of light was taken into account, the Impressionism of Monet and his friends. In sculpture it produced the waxworks of Madame Tussaud. These waxworks are a popular art form, strictly contemporary in appeal, making their maximum impact at the moment of creation. It is accepted that the wax effigy will eventually be melted down, and re-made into a less obsolete image.

It is almost impossible to lift this sort of sculpture to the fine art level; only Edgar Degas (1834–1917) did it, with his *Little Fourteen Year Old Dancer* which he showed at the Impressionist Exhibition in Paris in 1881. What we see of the sculpture today is a bronze cast, not the original, which looked very different. It was made of wax and coloured with paint, especially the face. All the clothes were real, not just some of them—the girl's linen bodice and satin shoes, as well as the muslin tutu and the hair ribbon. In fact Degas's *Little Dancer* came about as close to the waxwork as art can get and represents the extreme of naturalism in sculpture. Nobody could or did go further in this direction.

Edgar Degas *The Little Fourteen Year Old Dancer* 1881 (bronze with muslin skirt and satin hair-ribbon. 39" H) Courtesy of The Trustees of The Tate Gallery London

At precisely the same moment in Paris, however, another artist was exploring this problem of naturalism in sculpture, This was Auguste Rodin (1840–1917). A man of the people, Rodin succeeded in bringing life back to the art of sculpture. His work, impressive in itself, was full of suggestions that others were to take up. It is impossible to exaggerate his importance.

Rodin had shown at the Paris Salon of 1877 a figure of a young man rousing himself from sleep which was variously called *The Age of Bronze Man Awakening to Nature, The Creation of Man* The figure was so startlingly life-like that Rodin was accused of taking a cast of a living body, a practice considered reprehensible but furtively done by some of the Academicians and their aspirant followers. The accusation now seems ridiculous: the figure is not all that like a naked male body—neither proportions nor surfaces are particularly close to reality. But *The Age of Bronze* provided a sensational contrast to the average run of salon sculpture. The impression of life that it gave came from Rodin's genius and his understanding of the great sculpture of the past—especially of Michelangelo and the Greek and Gothic masters.

Rodin's most perfect naturalistic image of man. *The Age of Bronze,* was produced at the opening of his career. He went on to look for more meaningful images, and in doing so he opened up a whole range of new sculptural possibilities. He made the art of sculpture a more expressive one than had been thought possible. Two major projects pointed to new directions that have a vast twentieth-century progeny—*John the Baptist Preaching* and *Balzac.*

After *The Age of Bronze* Rodin decided to make an over-life size sculpture of *John the Baptist Preaching.* He had it ready in plaster for the 1880 salon, where it scored a considerable success. This finished work of the Saint moving forward to catch his audience's attention is less interesting to us today than the study which Rodin made for it, a sculpture generally known as *L'Homme qui Marche* (The Man Walking). The religious connotations are absent: there is no story to the sculpture. Rodin went on working at it for many years after he had exhibited *John the Baptist.* The original was probably accidentally damaged in his studio: the head and arm fell off, and Rodin accepted this—it helped to emphasize the massiveness of the torso proper, which he continued to build up.

Auguste Rodin *The Age of Bronze* 1877
(bronze, 71¼" H)
Courtesy of The Trustees of The Tate Gallery, London

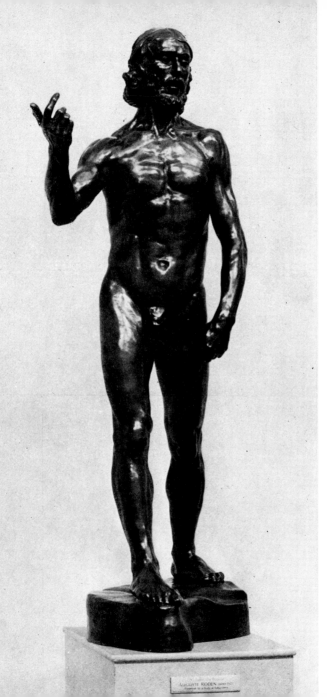

Rodin realized that the truncated image of man has a particular significance for us : we inevitably identify ourselves to some degree with any figurative sculpture, and we feel the loss of parts personally. The armless, headless, striding figure is more powerful and more poignant to us because of its maimed quality. It lacks the distinctive and personal parts of a man—the head and hands ; it could more nearly be an image of ourselves.

In the *Balzac* Rodin proposed another solution. He had been commissioned to make a monument of the great novelist in 1891, and after much preliminary study produced a massive pot-bellied nude figure that was somehow not quite suitable. So he threw a cloak around the body, hiding everything but the lumpy ungainly head, which emerges triumphantly from the enveloping mass of the drapery. The mystery that is lacking in the nude Balzac suddenly returned : here was an image of Balzac that was convincing in itself, and, because of the absence of any particularity, of much wider significance than is usually the case with public monuments.

In both works there is a degree of violence, a bursting vitality, that was characteristic of Rodin. His dying words might have expressed an admiration for the tranquil order of the paintings of his friend Puvis de Chavannes, but Rodin himself was a turbulent volcanic personality, in whose work the emotions are often about to erupt. Life, he seems to tell us through his sculpture, is a question of birth, love and death.

Themes of creation and destruction are fundamental to his work, and the union of man and woman is the crux around which all else revolves. It is a passionate, ecstatic union, that lifts both partners out of themselves. The figures flow into one another, the sculptural embodiment of the Bergsonian stream of life. Rodin sometimes called his lovers Paolo and Francesca, to make the subject publicly acceptable, but his intentions were quite obvious. His sensuality was unabashed, and the sculptures transmit his emotions frankly enough. Lacking reticence, he was bold enough to treat a subject almost untouched in Western art, though common in Indian sculpture, with which he was probably familiar. *The Kiss* is the public statement of this theme: less attractive to us today perhaps than Rodin's smaller and more personal sculptures, which are more in keeping with the privacy of the act itself.

Auguste Rodin *The Kiss* 1901–4
(Pentelicon marble, 71¾″ H)
Courtesy of The Trustees of The Tate Gallery, London

Auguste Rodin *Crouching Woman* c. 1891
(bronze, 20⅞″ H)
Courtesy of The Trustees of The Tate Gallery, London)

Aristide Maillol *Mediterranean* (or *The Thinker*) *c.* 1901
(plaster, about 40″ H)
© SPADEM Paris 1965

Rodin's emotionalism had resulted in some maltreatment of the body and his aggressive masculinity inevitably brought a reaction in favour of a body complete and composed. This is most clearly seen in the work of Aristide Maillol (1861–1944). Maillol began as a painter and tapestry designer: he turned to sculpture in his mid-thirties, making little statuettes of female figures in clay, terracotta and plaster. They were first exhibited in 1902 and, as images of man, at once provided an antithesis to Rodin. Fortunately, the two men could admire each other: 'I know nothing in modern sculpture so absolutely pure,' Rodin told a friend.

Maillol was almost exclusively concerned with the female figure. He wanted to present an ideal of classical tranquillity and serenity, totally opposed to the dynamic, dramatic expressionism of Rodin. His women exist outside time: they seem to have inhabited eternally the Mediterranean shores where Maillol himself chose to live. They never become too personal or individualized: 'the particular does not interest me,' said Maillol, 'what matters to me is the general idea.' And so he offers us another idealized image of woman.

The forms of the body are not abstracted; they are simplified to become rounded and massive; the compositions are closed and compact—a harmonious arrangement of sculptural rhythms, which always turn back on themselves and never break away. This gives the self-possessed, independent quality to the figures, which exist assertively in space as sculpture. There was little development in Maillol's work; his whole temperament was against change. But as he grew older the women became more grand and powerful, turning from innocent peasant girls into remote, mysterious nymphs and goddesses. Maillol seems to have wanted to create great Earth Mother images, offering them to us as objects for worship and veneration. There is a connection here, albeit an oblique one with some of Henry Moore's female figures.

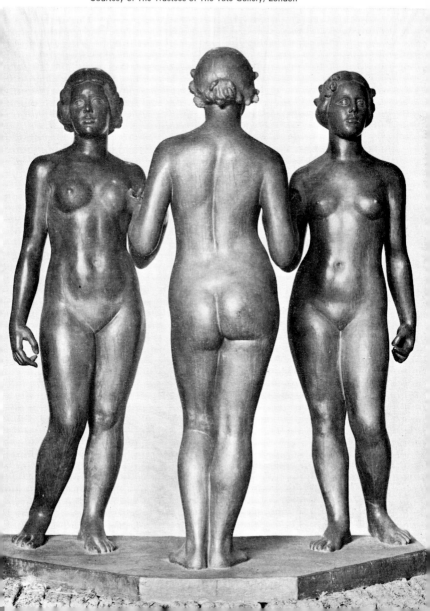

Like Maillol, Matisse (1869–1954), as a sculptor, was almost exclusively concerned with the female figure. His *œuvre* is very small—about seventy bronzes in all, most of them done in two short spells—in 1905–11 and 1925–30. For Matisse sculpture was an extension of his paintings, and he used it primarily to explore formal problems that were occupying him at the time. So there is a purity about Matisse's sculpture that comes from its total lack of emotional undertones.

In the early period Matisse, like many of his contemporaries at the time, was preoccupied with the question of abstraction. He takes a subject—a head, a reclining figure or, most remarkably, a woman's *back*—and proceeds to analyse it, articulating every plane and steadily exaggerating each feature (especially any asymmetrical elements), so that the impression is intensified to the point where the whole sculpture seems charged with vitality. And yet by comparison with Rodin or Maillol, Matisse is a very detached sculptor, standing back as it were, and not transmitting his own feelings through the figure he is making.

In the later work, it is true, this emotional coolness is much less marked. The tension is relaxed, and the latent sensuality in all of Matisse's painting and sculpture now comes forward. But for all the rich and formal inventiveness of such late sculptures as *The Tiara* (p. 30), something is missing. No doubt it is the absence of colour, for we can never forget that Matisse was one of the great colourists of all time, and colour provided the extra dimension that crowned his work.

Henri Matisse *The Back*, relief number 2 *c.* 1914
(bronze, 73⅝″ H)
Courtesy of The Trustees of The Tate Gallery, London

Henri Matisse *The Back*, relief number 3 *c.* 1914
(bronze, 73½″ H)
Courtesy of The Trustees of The Tate Gallery, London

Henri Matisse *The Back*, relief number 4 c. 1929
(bronze, 74″ H)
Courtesy of The Trustees of The Tate Gallery, London

The widespread trend towards abstraction that Matisse felt in the early years of the century was hostile to the sculptural treatment of the human image. As scientific knowledge of the universe advanced, so did man's importance seem to diminish. In the febrile and tense atmosphere that preceded the outbreak of the First World War, it was increasingly difficult for a young sculptor to present a convincing image of man. Violence in the air resulted either in a retreat from the figure, far more complete than anything ever anticipated, or in a maltreatment of it, as though in a cold, destructive rage.

Henri Matisse *The Tiara* 1930
(bronze, 8″ H)
Grosvenor Gallery, London

Pablo Picasso *Head* 1909
(bronze, 16¼" H)
© SPADEM Paris 1965

This is true of some futurist and cubist sculptors—Boccioni, for example, who submits the head of his mother to an almost total disintegration (p. 125). Picasso's cubist head of 1909 is more of an exercise perhaps—an investigation of the nature of solid form. But cubist sculpture lacks the logic of cubist painting. Picasso breaks up the head into flattened planes, but instead of arranging them on the flat canvas of the painting, proceeds to place them on what might be described as the egg-like abstracted shape of the head itself. And that mysterious mixing of the object with the space around it, familiar in cubist and futurist painting, is hardly possible in such a solidly material art as sculpture.

Of all the sculptors associated with the cubists—Picasso himself apart—the most gifted was certainly Jacques Lipchitz (born 1891). In his early work he mastered the new language of Cubism, turning it to valid three-dimensional ends. A Lipchitz cubist figure is a noble succession of regular solid forms, grouped together in a totally logical way. At a time when the carnage of the First World War was at its height, Lipchitz was starting from simple beginnings with a reconstruction of man. For him: 'Cubism was not a school, an aesthetic, or merely a discipline—it was a new view of the universe. Cubism sought a new way to represent nature, a manner adequate to the age. Cubism was essentially a search for a new syntax. Once this was arrived at there was no reason for not employing it in the expression of a full message. This is what I feel I have done and what I am still trying to do.'

Thus Jacques Lipchitz in 1945, when he had returned to the figure, after a period of experimental sculpture of remarkable originality which will be discussed later. In the later work he used the cubist freedom of representation in an attempt to revivify mythological and biblical themes. It was not a retreat into the past, for the contemporary relevance of subjects such as *The Rape of Europa* or *The Sacrifice of Hagar* must have been painfully obvious to a Russian Jew who had taken refuge in the United States after years of living in Paris.

Paradoxically, Lipchitz's personal involvement in his subject matter has in some ways been a barrier to the appreciation of his later sculpture. He treats familiar public themes, but in a language that was evolved with more private and intimate communication in mind, and a language to which he has himself given a very distinctive accent.

33

Ossip Zadkine *The Beautiful Servant* 1920
(bronze, $39\frac{2}{5}''$ H)

Another cubist-influenced sculptor whose career in many respects parallels that of Lipchitz is Ossip Zadkine (born 1890). He has never departed from the human figure, but Cubism showed him what liberties could be taken with the forms of the body for the sake of greater eloquence. The artist's eloquence has in fact been a major theme of Zadkine's sculpture: his many Orpheus figures show the poet as one with his lyre, and such symbolical subjects represent a major part of Zadkine's work.

Ossip Zadkine *Monument Commemorating the Destruction of Rotterdam*
1950–3
(bronze, 256″ H)

Henry Moore *Warrior with Shield* 1953–4 ▶
(bronze, 60″ H)

His masterpiece, however, is perhaps the *Monument Commemorating the Destruction of Rotterdam* (1950–3). Here, as in the case of Picasso's *Guernica,* the violence implied in the formal language of Cubism finds its emotional counterpart. Zadkine's figure is hacked about and pierced through the torso, and yet indomitably raises his arms in a great gesture of appeal and affirmation.

It is interesting to compare Zadkine's Rotterdam Memorial with Henry Moore's two warriors. For the *Warrior with Shield* (1953–4) has also been used as a war memorial—in Arnhem—and the image it presents is a very similar one, of the battered and mutilated man refusing to concede defeat.

If Moore's Warrior lacks the rhetoric of Zadkine's and is less suitable for a public monument, it is, as sculpture, more com-

Henry Moore *Warrior with Shield* 1953–4
(bronze, 60″ H)

Henry Moore *Falling Warrior* 1956–7
(bronze, 58″ L)
detail overleaf ▶

pletely convincing. The body is more savagely truncated than anything in Rodin, and we immediately feel the loss of the limbs as a personal loss. The cleft head seems to have been divided by some great axe-blow, its absence of distinguishing personal features lifts the figure into the category of a god. Yet certain parts of it are unmistakably human—the one surviving hand that shelters behind the shield, or the broad shoulders that remind us of the Warrior's strength.

Such details as these at once arouse our empathetic responses, and we are involved in the sculpture in the remarkably intimate way mentioned at the beginning of this chapter. This is even more the case in the *Falling Warrior* of 1956–7. It is impossible to look at this work and not have oneself the sensation of falling. Without any sort of intellectual process intervening one simply gets the feeling inside one's own body of the buttocks and back about to crash down. It is almost too painful to contemplate, and the Warrior's predicament is acutely brought home to us. Why there should be this bodily contact with the sculpture is only partly explicable, the consummate mastery of the sculptor prevents us seeing exactly how it is done. But the feeling is real enough, and it reminds us again of the particular advantages the sculptor has in being able to use the human body as the vehicle for artistic expression.

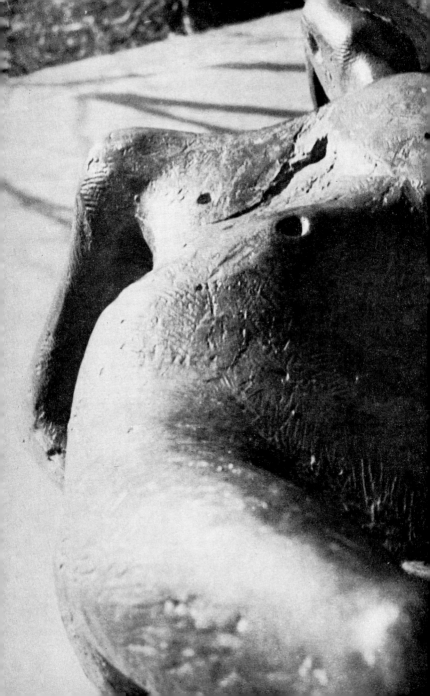

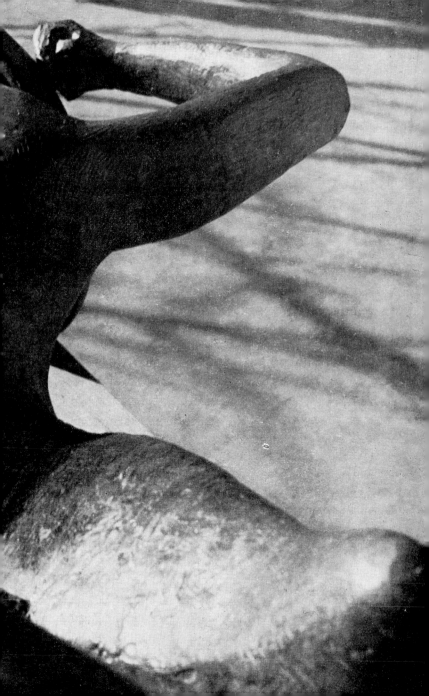

Another example that springs to mind is the Italian sculptor, Marino Marini (born 1901). A little younger than Moore (born 1898), he has constantly returned throughout his career to the theme of the horseman. It may seem surprising that an Italian in the machine age should turn to the traditional equestrian figure, but the very lack of any contemporary relevance in the man on horseback gives a timeless and universal quality to the image.

In Marini's sculptures the rider assumes an increasingly precarious position on the back of the horse. Losing his balance, he begins to fall, but as he does so he seems increasingly to become fused with the horse, so that man and animal are one. His back rests on the horse's back, and is a part of it; and the horse falls too, stumbling to its knees, or rearing up into the air.

◀ **Marino Marini** *Horseman* 1949
(bronze, 12" H)

Marino Marini *Small Horseman* 1950
(bronze, 11" H)

The image of unified horse and rider has allowed Marini to pursue a series of variations on a dynamic and expressive shape. He possesses that same grasp of the three-dimensionality of sculpture that is so remarkable in Henry Moore; he may lack Moore's variety, but he shares his vitality, and even the near symmetry of his sculptures gives them an imposing and powerful presence.

One would imagine that Marini intends some sort of philosophical meaning from his horse and rider image. The act of balancing crystallizes in itself the act of living—and it is significant that when Marini has chosen other subjects for sculpture he has made jugglers and dancers, where the balance idea also comes into play. Even when all seems trouble-free, disaster can so easily strike, and the final impression of Marini's work is of an unbearable mounting tension only just held back by a classical gravity and calm.

These same undertones are very much evident in the sculpture of Alberto Giacometti, born in Italian-speaking Switzerland in the same year as Marini. Their forms may be totally different, but the two men share a sense of history, both of the distant past and of the present. The savagery and terror of the world they have lived in makes itself felt in their work, albeit indirectly.

Giacometti made his reputation as a surrealist sculptor in the Paris of the late twenties and early thirties. He created objects: sometimes they were fetish-like, sometimes they had the visionary quality of a remembered dream, like his *Palace at 4 a.m.* (p. 89) a construction made out of wood, glass, wire and string—the sort of thing only possible at a time when experiment with new materials was in favour, as we shall see in a later chapter.

But Giacometti gave up all such experiment, and went back to the human image. It was a difficult and even heroic decision, not a renunciation of the past, but an acceptance of the necessity to move forward. As he himself noted in an autobiographical fragment: 'I saw afresh the bodies that attracted me in life and the

Alberto Giacometti *Venise IV* 1957
(bronze, 45⅝" H)
Galerie Maeght, Paris

Alberto Giacometti *Man Pointing* 1947
(bronze, 70" H)
Courtesy of The Trustees of The Tate Gallery, London

abstract forms which I felt were true in sculpture. But I wanted the one without losing the other (very briefly put).'

Giacometti began by working from the model again, then from memory: 'But wanting to create from memory what I had seen, to my terror the sculptures became smaller and smaller; they only had a likeness when very small, yet their dimensions revolted me ...' Here was his dilemma: 'A large figure seemed to me untrue and a small one intolerable', and this was only solved by making the figures long and slender, and in this way the characteristic Giacometti form was evolved.

These tall figures of Giacometti's are full of paradox. Stylized to a degree, they can also be representational in a most striking fashion. Their encrusted surfaces—they sometimes seem to have just been dug out of the earth—repel us, and yet their insubstantiality allows us to take possession of them. As Giacometti says, 'Our eye can absorb an object only if its measure is reduced.' And again, 'I have never regarded my figures as a compact mass, but as transparent constructions. It was not the outward form of human beings which interested me, but the effect they have had on my inner life.'

This rather cryptic statement encourages us to probe the meaning of Giacometti's figures. He is evidently concerned with human relationships—both in his groups of figures and in the single images, which, like the *Man Pointing*, at once implicate the spectator. As one might expect from a friend of Jean Paul Sartre's, the philosophy is a pessimistic, existentialist one, and the sculpture leaves one with a strong impression of the loneliness of man and the emptiness of existence. It is not a comfortable message, any more than Marini's is; and it is less positive than Moore's.

The way that Giacometti caught the particular mood of Paris in the forties shows clearly the continuing validity that the image of man offers the sculptor. When it came to it, there was no sculptor who caught that *Angst*-ridden mood in comparable degree. Younger and more abstract sculptors produced more original images, and though some carried great conviction at the time, they have lasted less well than Giacometti's tall figurines. The modern sculptor has a range of possibilities before him undreamed of in any previous age. The language of sculpture is today richer than it has ever been. And yet when this has been said, can it be doubted that the image of man will remain the sculptor's central preoccupation, something to which he must always return?

Alberto Giacometti *The Forest* (*Seven Figures and a Head*) 1950
(bronze, 18¾″ H)

47

2 Pure form and expressive surface

When the subject matter of sculpture declines in importance, attention is concentrated on abstract qualities. Chief of these are form and surface.

The form of sculpture—its shape and structure, not the material from which it is composed—is, of course, fundamental. As we have seen already, sculpture is an art that, like us, exists in space. So our awareness of sculpture is, as Herbert Read has pointed out,* on a very elemental and primitive level. We pick up a pebble because its shape pleases us; we hold it cupped in a hand, feeling the shape through our fingers, and there is something peculiarly satisfying about this experience. Psychologists have been quick to tell us why, advancing reasons that refer to infantile and pre-natal memories. This may well be true; but what really matters is the existence of this basic response between us and the solid, sculptural form—because upon this the whole art of sculpture is founded.

Having said this, one must quickly add that appreciation of three-dimensional form, though fundamental, becomes very subtle and refined, as the form itself grows in complexity and art. There is all the difference between a pebble and a Michelangelo; and there is a considerable difference between a pebble and a Brancusi, the sculptor who will figure most prominently in this chapter.

The point is that appreciation of sculpture, like the appreciation of any art, makes certain demands on the spectator. We have to train ourselves to an awareness of the sculpture as an object, we have to savour its essentially three-dimensional quality, and this means looking at the sculpture hard and long, and moving around it, taking up different positions, so that we begin to grasp it as a solid shape.

It is necessary to stress this, because some people with a keen visual sensibility and a profound understanding of painting never really come to grips with sculpture. One of the greatest art critics of all time—Baudelaire—is a case in point. Admittedly the mid-nineteenth century was a period of almost unequalled sculptural decadence, and one can sympathize with Baudelaire when he entitled the sculpture section of his review of the Salon

* Especially in *The Art of Sculpture:* the Mellon lectures of 1954 (Faber 1956), but our appreciation of sculpture today owes a great debt to Herbert Read's writing.

of 1846: 'Why sculpture is boring'. He found it a subsidiary art, the inferior complement to architecture and painting, but the two reasons for this that he gave now astonish us. A work of sculpture exhibits too many surfaces at once, he says; if there was a single viewpoint, as with a painting, it would be less arbitrary. It is a physical object, he goes on, and this allows less scope to the imagination than something we peer at through the picture frame. Baudelaire has here isolated two of the distinctive qualities of sculpture; and modern sculptors have turned them to advantage and made them the virtues of the art, not the vices. We judge a great sculptor—a Michelangelo or a Moore—by the rich variety of expressive viewpoints that his work offers us, and the fact that it exists tangibly in our space makes it more mysterious and exciting to the imagination, not less.

One forgives Baudelaire, because none of his contemporaries could show him the true nature and possibilities of sculpture. He was acute enough to realize the primitive, barbaric quality

Constantin Brancusi *Sleeping Muse I* 1908
(marble, 15¾" L)
Art Museum of the Rumanian People's Republic, Bucharest

inherent in what he called 'a Carib art', and he even prophesies, quite correctly, a blossoming of sculpture at the end of the century when the great age of French painting begins to decline. The difficulties he experienced are, however, still with us, and the fact that any illustration of sculpture inevitably falsifies confirms this. (The reproductions in this book, for example, show only the silhouetted forms of three-dimensional objects, seen from a single arbitrary view-point, and sometimes illuminated in an over-dramatic or a deadening manner.)

It was the supreme importance of Constantin Brancusi (1876–1957) that he drew attention to the essentially sculptural qualities of the art. To quote Henry Moore's tribute : 'Since Gothic, European sculpture had become overgrown with moss, weeds—all sorts of surface excrescences which completely concealed shape. It has been Brancusi's special mission to get rid of this undergrowth and to make us once more shape conscious.'

Brancusi did this in a direct and unpretentious way. He had the advantages of remarkable natural talent—as his early figurative works show—and the temperament of a simple, untroubled and yet deep-thinking man. He was born in the Carpathian mountains of Rumania, the son of a peasant, and spent his early years as a shepherd boy. He had no formal education, and did not learn to read and write until he was eighteen. His first training was at a craft school, and though he went on to study sculpture in the Academies of Bucharest and Paris, he retained the manner and approach to his work of the artisan, rather than that of the artist.

He had arrived in Paris in 1904, when he was twenty-eight, knowing that he must come and settle in the place where the art of sculpture was being reborn. He was attracted by Rodin : 'He transformed everything,' he later said. 'His influence was and remains immense.' Rodin admired the sculpture of the young Rumanian when he saw it at the 1907 Salon, and asked him if he would like to work with him in his studio. But Brancusi, without hostility and without offending Rodin, turned down the invitation : 'I refused to work for him, for nothing grows under big trees,' he said.

Brancusi was quite right. As we have already seen, the younger sculptors in Paris—notably Maillol and Matisse—had taken a decisive step towards a less romantic, more abstract conception of sculpture than Rodin's. They were treating the human figure with considerable liberty, feeling free to simplify and rearrange the
50

forms to make a more harmonious (Maillol) or a more expressive (Matisse) image. The general swing away from naturalism was already clear in Rodin, of course, but it became progressively more pronounced between 1900 and 1915, and no one exemplifies this tendency better than Brancusi.

He had first explicitly to reject the whole West European sculptural tradition that culminates in Michelangelo and Rodin, and to which he himself had at first adhered: 'They worked in beefsteak,' he would say; 'I too worked in beefsteak—anatomies, representations, copies.' The problem for Brancusi was to get to the heart of the matter: 'It is not the outward form that is real, but the essence of things . . . It is impossible to express anything real by imitating the outer surface of things.'

In his search for the essential, Brancusi simplified until he reached a pure and perfect form. He takes the human head, for example, calling it at first *Sleeping Muse*—reminding us that there are classical prototypes for such a sculpture, though the

Constantin Brancusi *Sleeping Muse II* 1910
(bronze, 11″ L)
Courtesy of The Art Institute of Chicago, Arthur Jerome Eddy Memorial Collection

treatment of the head emerging from the rough-cut stone is pure Rodin. In the second *Sleeping Muse* of 1910 the head has in fact emerged, and rests, a solid ovoid form, on the ground. The features of nose and eyes and mouth are present, but heavily stylized; they have an ethereal quality, as if in another world. The Muse's head now makes us think of the severed head of Orpheus, which went on singing after the poet's physical death—an image of the artist's immortality won by his art, which, once created, is outside time. If the song is meaningful, it will be heard for ever.

In the general atmosphere of revolutionary extremism that characterized Paris immediately before the outbreak of the First World War, Brancusi was able to go still further. The *New Born* of 1915 is the same head, now reduced to a pure form—its essence, if you like—reminding one that external reality is superficial compared to the depths of the inner life. The ovoid form which

Constantin Brancusi *The New Born* 1915
(marble, 8½" L)
Philadelphia Museum of Art, The Louise and Walter Arensberg Collection

underlies the head now takes it over: it is not a dead, mechanical shape but a live one. We inevitably see it as an egg, as well as a head; and the egg is a symbol of life of immeasurable antiquity and universal validity. Its Christian use in the Easter celebrations is familiar to all of us, and that the association is deliberate may be supported by Brancusi's change of title to *The New Born*.

Brancusi went even further with his refinement of the head shape in a sculpture of 1924 which he called *The Beginning of the World*. All the surface features of the face have disappeared; this is Brancusi's final statement, his essence of the human head. He also called this work *Sculpture for the Blind*, as if to remind us that our appreciation of sculpture can be tactile as well as visual. We feel the pebble in our closed fist, or we want to stroke and touch the smooth forms of such sculpture, to enlarge our knowledge of them. The eye alone is insufficient.

Constantin Brancusi *Sculpture for the Blind* (*The Beginning of the World*) 1924
(marble, 12″ L)
Philadelphia Museum of Art, The Louise and Walter Arensberg Collection

Brancusi went on to provide the essence of other human and animal forms besides the head. He could never treat the whole human body in this way, but he took part of it—the head and shoulders and hands (in some of the *Mlle Pogany* and *Princesse X* sculptures), or the lower part of the legless body (in the Torsos of the Girl and of the Young Man). With animals his success was more complete—the fish, the bird and the seal, for example, are probably his most approachable and acceptable works, where the basic nature of his sculpture must be obvious to anyone. There is a certain naïvety, even a simple-mindedness, about his approach; but simplicity was of basic importance to Brancusi, if the essentially religious message of his sculpture was to be made clear.

Constantin Brancusi *Torso of a Young Girl* 1922
(onyx, 13¾″ H)
Philadelphia Museum of Art, A. E. Gallatin Collection

Constantin Brancusi *Torso of a Young Man* 1922
(maple, 19″ H)
Philadelphia Museum of Art, The Louise and Walter Arensberg Collection

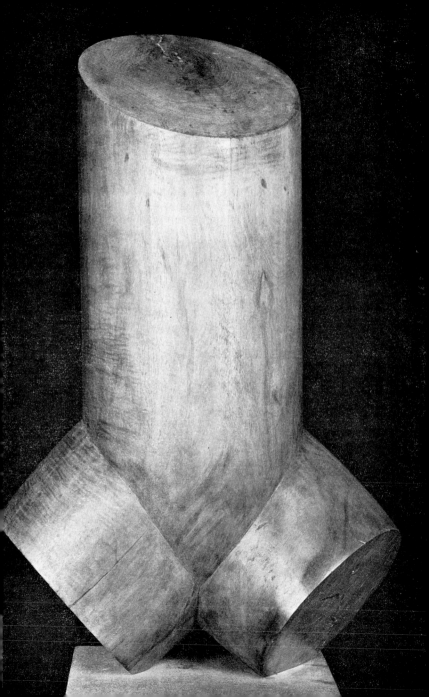

Constantin Brancusi *Fish* 1926
(bronze, 31½" H)
Collection E. J. Power, London

Constantin Brancusi *The Seal (The Miracle) 1943*
(grey marble, 62" H)
National Museum of Modern Art, Paris

Even the animals take on a spiritual significance. One of the first birds that Brancusi made was called *Maistra*, after the bird in a Rumanian tale who guides the lover through the forest to the place where the princess is imprisoned. Thus the bird is our guide, leading us upwards towards spiritual liberation. Brancusi said of the *Bird in Space* of 1925 that it was a 'project that should be enlarged to fill the vault of heaven'; and he was delighted when the Maharajah of Indore bought three birds and invited him to build a Temple of Deliverance—a house of meditation, in the form of a cross, where the birds in polished bronze and in black and white marble would be placed so as to be reflected in the still

Constantin Brancusi *Bird in Space* 1919
(bronze, 54″ H) ▶
Museum of Modern Art, New York

Constantin Brancusi *Maistra* 1915
(bronze, 25″ H)
Collection Peggy Guggenheim, Venice

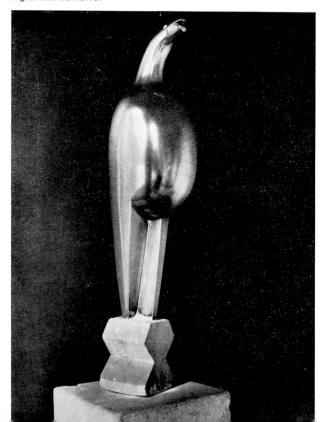

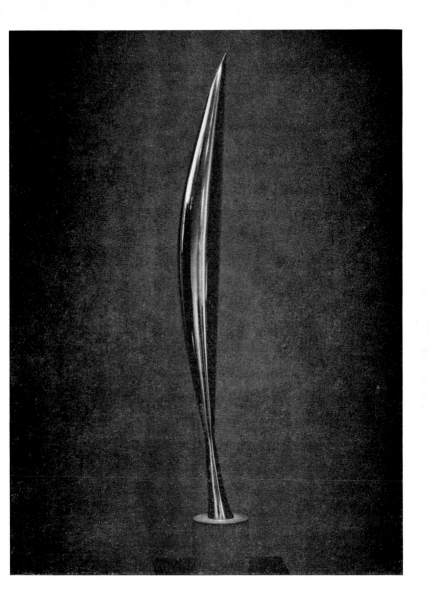

surface of a pool. This project was never realized, but Brancusi did make a garden at Tirgu Jiu in his native Rumania where an endless column—the abstract equivalent of the soaring bird—rises a hundred feet up into the sky.

There are other aspects of Brancusi's sculpture which will be discussed in the next chapters—his primitivistic wood carvings and his craftsman's sensibility to materials. What matters here is the drive away from representation towards the pure, ideal form ; and the philosophic justification that was advanced for it. All the great figures of the first generation of abstract artists—Mondrian, Kandinsky, Malěvich—seem to have needed some sort of mystical faith to defend their work against the accusation, made by Picasso and his friends for example, that abstract art could only be decorative art. Brancusi's sculpture is, strictly speaking, not so much abstract as abstracted : it is the *essence* of some existing human or animal form that he strives for. There was a positive justification for this search: 'Balanced forms and proportions are the great Yes : through them we can get to know ourselves.' Brancusi was much affected by his reading of oriental religious and philosophic texts : his whole life and art were directed towards the attainment of that state of spiritual enlightenment beyond the self which is called *Nirvana*. Without necessarily sharing this aim, we can nevertheless feel the force of his works as objects for meditation and contemplation—no new purpose of art, but something at times forgotten in the twentieth century.

Brancusi's influence on modern sculpture has been enormous. As Henry Moore said, he made people 'shape conscious', and opened our eyes to the beauty and meaning of pure forms. Confronted by the mystery of a Brancusi sculpture one is thrown back to a basic response. Though one can understand certain temperaments finding it totally unsympathetic, appreciation of his work is a touchstone of one's appreciation of the art of sculpture itself.

Constantin Brancusi *Endless Column* 1937
(steel, 100' H)
Tirgu Jiu, Rumania

It was inevitable that younger sculptors should be impressed by Brancusi's example, and I want to conclude this section by discussing two of them, Jean Arp and Barbara Hepworth. These three artists have some common ground, but each in fact takes up an individual and distinct position.

The forms of Arp (born 1887) may have a superficial resemblance to those of Brancusi, but their derivation is entirely different. A look at Arp's background soon shows why. Until about 1930, when he was forty-three, Arp had done no sculpture in the round at all. He was a poet, a painter and a maker of painted wood relief constructions. He had been a leading member of Dada and surrealist groups, and allowed his art to be shaped by the forces of the unconscious. A whole new world had been opened up to art.

The sculptures which Arp began to make in the early 1930s were free forms that had no direct reference to anything outside themselves. Arp liked to say that they had grown naturally in his hands: 'Art is a fruit growing out of man like the fruit out of a plant, like the child out of the mother,' to quote the original wording of his best-known maxim.

There must be a point of departure for any form, however, and in Arp's case we can trace the *Configurations* and *Evocations*, as he called them, back to the early reliefs. The forms in these are often arranged 'according to the laws of chance' and their very shape may be dictated by creative accident. Arp would throw a piece of coiled rope on to the ground, and then draw the shape it assumed when it fell: that shape would then be reproduced in a relief. Such a process—and there are other comparable ones— is not altogether arbitrary; there is an element of conscious selection on the artist's part when he decides a shape is worth drawing, and he uses his aesthetic judgment if he develops the shape still further. What he has been presented with is in fact a totally free form (albeit conditioned by such factors as the length of the rope), non-descriptive and non-representational—something which he can then feed, as it were, into his imaginative processes.

Jean Arp *Shepherd of the Clouds* 1953
(bronze, 63″ H)
Kröller-Müller Museum, Otterlo

Jean Arp *Bird Tripod*
(bronze, 30″ H)
Collection Mrs Keiller, Kingston Hill

Jean Arp *Undulating Threshold* 1960
(bronze, 25⅝″ L)
Galerie Denise René, Paris

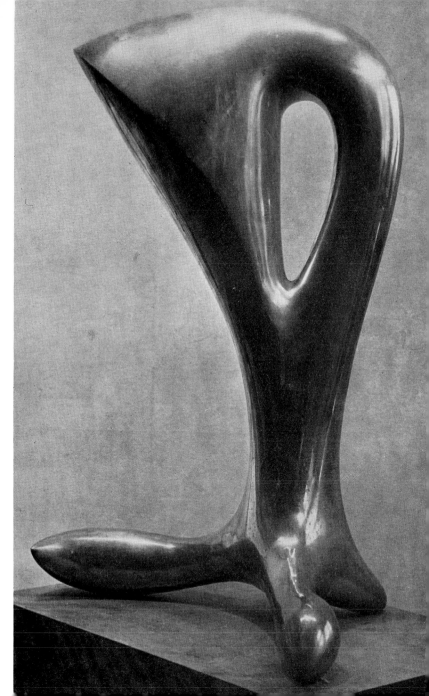

There is nothing remarkable about the way that this is done—artists have always drawn on a random collection of visual impressions, but their art is basically self-generating, one work leading them inevitably to the next. This is precisely true of Arp's sculpture : the formal repertoire is consistent—all the shapes have an organic quality, and make one feel they are what they are because they have grown in that way. So we may say that his art is about growth and change. It is harmonious, as is Brancusi's, but the harmony is explicitly with the natural world. Arp is in love with nature, recognizing its healing power—there is a spirituality about his sculpture which relates not to oriental mysticism but to the nature-worshipping, Wordsworthian pantheism of the Romantics. 'Man must re-enter Nature,' he once said, and this seems to imply a certain submerging of the human into the natural. Of course certain of Arp's organic forms have suggested the human figure : he has accepted this, and called them Torso or Head or whatever is appropriate. These are not the most successful of his sculptures, I think, because the form is so plainly more vegetable—more fruit-like—than it is human, and this sets up a basic contradiction. We lose too that feeling of being offered a secret insight into the world of nature that Arp's work can give us : he is obsessed with particular shapes that recur again and again, as though their appearance is governed by laws of natural growth, and it is these images that stand out as the most potent and mysterious of his sculpture.
68

With Barbara Hepworth (born 1903), who belongs to a still younger generation, we complete this particular circle and return to the human image that this whole development began by rejecting. For her sculpture is essentially humanist in character; though it does not attempt the imitation of the figure, it is pre-occupied with man. She has written: 'I hope to discover some absolute essence in sculptural terms giving the quality of human relationship.' She was able in the 1930s, under the influence of Brancusi, to create pure abstract forms that existed in their own right without reference to anything outside themselves. They were neither extreme simplifications of parts of the body, as with Brancusi, nor were they the kind of organic forms that we find in Arp's sculpture. They possessed a cool mathematical purity and approached the shapes of geometry, while remaining un-mistakably works of art. It was the quality of the materials carved—stone or wood—that confirmed this. At the same time the human reference was not far away. This is something almost inescapable, however abstract in intention the sculpture may be. One has only to stick a pole in the ground for it to suggest a figure, so strong is our desire to relate any unfamiliar man-sized object to ourselves. Slowly in Hepworth's case the three basic forms of her sculpture crys-tallized. She has described their human significance: 'The forms which have had special meaning for me since childhood have been the standing form (which is the translation of my feeling towards the human being standing in a landscape); the two forms (which is the tender relationship of one living thing beside another); and the closed form . . . which translates for me the association and meaning of gesture in landscape; in the repose of a mother and child, or the feeling of the embrace of living things, either in nature or in the human spirit.'

So we find, throughout Hepworth's sculpture, abstract forms used as human equivalents. This allows her to express a certain view of the relationships between man and nature, and between man and his fellows, that is positive and affirmative. These forms also take on a symbolic quality, and, as the titles often suggest, assume the character of an icon or a totem. This will be discussed in the next chapter, because it involves us in the whole idea of magic and metamorphosis.

Barbara Hepworth *Two Figures* (*Menhirs*) 1955
(teak, 54" H)
Collection S. B. Smith, Chicago

The idea of an expressive surface to sculpture is a much less complicated one, and can be discussed briefly. It is self-evident that with the increasing concern for the sculpture as an object, the actual surface, as well as the form itself, should assume greater prominence. Like so much in modern sculpture, this, too, goes back to Rodin.

Rodin noticed how the surface of a Greek marble statue was not smooth, but made up of innumerable slight projections and depressions which showed up only in strong light. It was this uneven surface, he realized, that gave Greek work a vitality that no neo-classical imitator could achieve. Following this example, Rodin

◀ **Barbara Hepworth** *Curved Form* (*Delphi*) 1955
(scented guarea, 42″ H)
Collection The Artist

Barbara Hepworth *Discs in Echelon* 1935–59
(bronze, 20¾″ L)
Collection The Artist

Barbara Hepworth *Three Forms in Echelon* 1964
(slate, 19¼″ H)
Marlborough Fine Art Ltd, London

began to exaggerate the modelled surfaces of his own work; he wanted also to catch the flickering effects as light and shadow played over his figures. We do well to remember that Rodin was of the same generation as the Impressionists—he was in fact born two days before Monet—and it was an awareness of light more than anything else that revolutionized their painting.

The danger for the sculptor, however, is that light so easily dissolves form, and formless sculpture is almost a contradiction in itself. To introduce into sculpture any style evolved primarily for painting brings with it acute problems, and the man who made the most determined effort to create an *impressionist* sculpture —the Italian, Medardo Rosso (1858–1928)—was reduced to inactivity. Rosso's work does, however, remind us of the dilemma: it polarizes itself into the opposites of pure form and surface. He produces either heads of a simplified oval shape that seem to anticipate Brancusi, or flat reliefs that make sense only when seen from one point of view, and have only a limited three-dimensionality.

74

Relief sculpture is perhaps the logical consequence of a preoccupation with surface. At its extreme, the predetermined rectangular form of a picture is accepted, so is the situation of something that hangs on a wall. It is a general characteristic of recent painting in Europe that the surface assumes greater importance—this is in part a consequence of abstraction and the abandonment of illusionism. The picture is not pretending to be anything, it simply exists. And there is a point here where the two arts meet : it is difficult to say whether someone like the Rumanian-born Swiss, Zoltan Kemeny (1907–1965), is a painter or a relief sculptor. What he has certainly achieved is a new and original synthesis of the two arts.

Zoltan Kemeny *Armourium: Sculpture Number 123* (detail) 1961
(red copper, 78¾″ H)
Collection The Artist

More generally important has been the sensitivity towards surface effects that younger sculptors have shown. Men like César (born 1921) and Eduardo Paolozzi (born 1924) have been ready to use the most improbable objects to enliven the surfaces of their sculptures, yet they have remained unquestionably in the field of 'solid sculpture'. It is a question of a younger generation tackling with assurance a problem that defeated many of their elders. One of the reasons for this was that they benefited from the somewhat changed atmosphere that came with the new attitude to materials, and this, too, is something that will be discussed in a later chapter.

Eduardo Paolozzi *Large Frog* 1958
(bronze, 34″ L)
Collection The British Council

César *Grand Panneau* (detail) 1958
(welded iron, 72¾" H)
Courtesy of The Trustees of The Tate Gallery, London

3 Magic and metamorphosis

Nothing is more fundamental to the art of sculpture than the idea of metamorphosis. It is intrinsic in the magic of the art itself—the transformation of anonymous matter into something cherished eternally for certain extrinsic qualities that the sculptor has managed to put into it. Or at least this has been the sculptor's intention, for often, despite his skill and high ambitions, the matter remains inert, the sculpture is dead and lifeless—nothing more than a heavy lump of stone or wood or bronze. Why this should be is sometimes difficult to say—as with any work of art there is a final mystery about why it should have the power to hold and move us that it does.

This transmutation idea is perhaps more obvious in sculpture than in the other arts—even painting and architecture—because of the very materiality of sculpture. And it is for this reason that sculptors have always been quick to exploit it and extend it, and make it an essential part of the sculpture's meaning. This has been much more obvious in the twentieth century than in earlier periods, though metamorphoses did exist in the past. One of Bernini's most beautiful sculptures is of Daphne being pursued by Apollo. At the moment the god seizes her, the nymph is changed into a bay tree. With virtuoso delight, Bernini shows us the moment of transformation, with the laurel sprigs sprouting from Daphne's body.

This image of Bernini's might serve as an archetype for much of the sculpture of our time. For the idea of a metamorphosis has been crucial. We have seen it already in Brancusi's abstracting of the sleeping head into an egg-like shape which he then calls *The New Born*; but other sculptors come much closer to capturing the actual moment of change, as Bernini does.

The first to spring to mind is Germaine Richier, who died in 1959 at the early age of fifty-four. She was a Provençale, with a powerful and sometimes sinister imagination which only came to life in the dark and threatening years of the 1940s. 'My subjects belong to the world of metamorphosis,' she once wrote, and this is confirmed by the titles she gave her works—*Homme-Forêt, Homme-Oiseau, Homme-L'Orage, La Montagne, La Feuille* and so on.

In each of Richier's sculptures we have something that is half human, and half something else. It may be part animal or insect— a bat or a spider—and the figure takes on the disturbing qualities we associate with such creatures. More often, the transformation is between man and something totally alien. *L'Eau* is clearly enough a woman, until the top of the sculpture is reached, and there the head is replaced by the handles and neck of an amphora. *Don Quixote of the Forest* stands with his lance ready to tilt at the windmills, but as we come closer to him we see that his excoriated legs are the rough and peeling bark of a tree. *La Feuille* is an emaciated young girl, but she is also a frail and withered leaf.

The human part of these sculptures provides our point of contact, of identification, and then leads us into the strange world of the imagination in which the sculptor lived, and out of which her figures and animals grew. It was a remarkably individual and self-contained world, suggesting human life at its most primitive and elemental, when man was closest to the animals and to nature. The primal forest is always crowding in; dwarfed by such savage surroundings man is reduced to insect stature, and, by a reversal of nature, the ants and the grasshoppers, bats and spiders, assume superhuman size.

In many cases too there is an atmosphere of decay and decrepitude: an ever-present sense of death haunts Richier's sculpture. At times a figure seems to have been dug directly out of the earth; only the skeleton remains, the putrefied remainder has rotted away. What could be more foreboding than the death's-head image of the *Berger des Landes*? One feels the sculptor must have a more than normal insight into a world of horror and darkness, and it is hard not to see in her work an indirect reaction to the terrible experiences of war and Nazi tyranny.

Germaine Richier *L'Eau* (*L'Amphore*) 1944
(bronze, 57½″ H)
Courtesy of The Trustees of The Tate Gallery, London

Germaine Richier *Small Grasshopper* 1946
(bronze, 10½″ H)
Hanover Gallery, London

83

To turn from Richier to Picasso is to move from night into sunlight, and yet the idea of metamorphosis is basic to the sculpture of both of them. Picasso is a great sculptor—it is not inconceivable that the time will come when his activities as a sculptor in the second part of his life are regarded as of more consequence than his later paintings. But like other painter-sculptors (as we have already seen) Picasso has turned to sculpture from time to time when, for one reason or another, he needed to move into the third dimension; and his career has an inconsequential quality about it. Picasso's sculpture sparkles with bright ideas—enough to have kept many a lesser man occupied for the whole of a working lifetime.

Nothing has been more remarkable than Picasso's use of found objects as the raw material for his sculpture. In some respects we anticipate the next chapter, but the use made of this material is relevant here. Picking up the broken parts of a bicycle, he joined the saddle to the handlebars to make the head of a bull: with the help of a feather duster, a child's scooter could be turned into a wading bird: a tea infuser or a coffee grinder, taken to pieces, provided the parts for a head or a figure.

Any sort of rubbish could, in Picasso's hands, be transmuted into art. His apparently arrogant and over-confident assertion: 'I do not seek: I find', is better seen as an extension of the surrealist doctrine that anything can be made into art, given that we possess the necessary magic powers. And Picasso is the supreme example of artist as magician. Endlessly inventive, his incongruous associations take on a life of their own: the tricks are dazzling and clever and full of humour and *joie de vivre*. As a sculptor Picasso relaxes; the general tone and feeling is noticeably more lighthearted than in his paintings.

Pablo Picasso *Head of Bull, Metamorphosis* 1943
Collection The Artist (construction, 16″ H)
© SPADEM Paris 1965

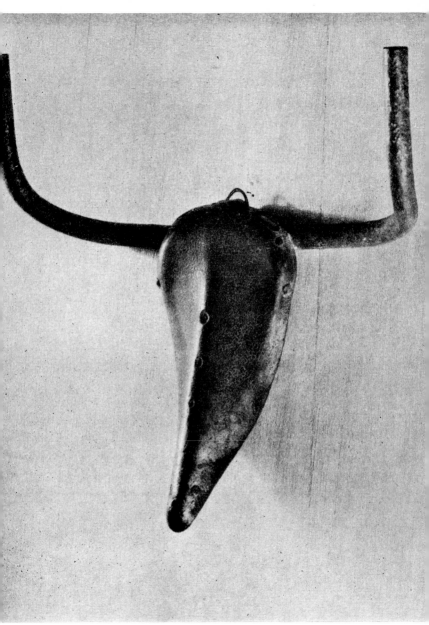

Pablo Picasso *Scooter and Feather* 1942
(iron construction, 25″ H)
Collection The Artist

Pablo Picasso *Baboon and Young* 1951
(bronze, 21″ H)
© SPADEM 1965 Paris

Not all of Picasso's sculpture is constructed out of found objects. He has also used metal wire, and plaster that has been moulded and cast in bronze. Great lumps of plaster have been thrown together to make the heads and bodies of female figures. But this more serious, more monumental side to Picasso's activity as a sculptor is a very incomplete one, and there are certain paintings which suggest possibilities that Picasso himself never pursued into the third dimension. In them Picasso gives us what looks like pictures of sculpture. I am thinking in particular of a series of paintings Picasso made in 1930 when he was planning a huge monument to the poet Apollinaire, which was to be set up on the promenade overlooking the Mediterranean at Cannes. Picasso took the female figure, but instead of treating it naturalistically he isolated a number of simple forms, clearly related to the body, and then reassembled them into a coherent whole. Sometimes these forms strongly resemble bones, which are then juxtaposed with the globe of the woman's breast or the curved shape of the buttock. Such independent elements, placed in conjunction with each other, add up to an image of monumental power and dignity.

Pablo Picasso *Head of a Woman* 1931
(iron construction, 40" H)
Collection, The Artist

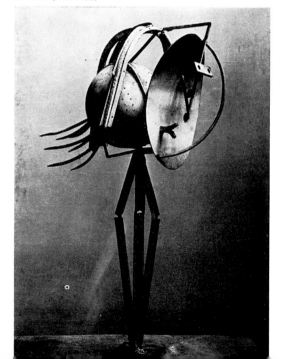

Alberto Giacometti *The Palace at 4 a.m.* 1933
(construction in wood, glass, wire and string, 28″ L)
Collection, The Museum of Modern Art, New York

In fact, no such monument to Apollinaire was ever erected—
the whole project was probably totally impracticable from a
structural point of view, but Picasso was not hampered by such
considerations. It remains an extraordinarily imaginative conception of what sculpture might be made to do, and one of the young
sculptors who was stimulated by such visions was Henry Moore.
For the twenties and thirties were a time when the movement
away from naturalism had gone so far that any kind of sculptural
fantasy was possible, to a degree that became almost out of hand.
The surrealist emphasis on the dream world allowed such remarkable inventions as Giacometti's *Palace at 4 a.m.,* but as
Giacometti himself soon found, this kind of thing is a sculptural
dead end that leads nowhere. What was necessary was a discip-
lined reappraisal of the whole art of sculpture—what its true
nature was, and what possibilities were most rewarding to pursue.
And this, Henry Moore, more than any of his contemporaries, was
to provide.

A statement, first published in 1934, when Moore was thirty-five, is clear evidence of this. It was later called *The Sculptor's Aims*, and in it Moore tried to define those qualities in sculpture which are of fundamental importance. First comes truth to material : 'Every material has its own individual qualities . . . stone, for example, is hard and concentrated and should not be falsified to look like soft flesh . . . It should keep its hard tense stoniness.'

Now there are implications in this remark about the demands a particular material makes, and these will be discussed in the next chapter. It is at the same time, however, a declaration by the sculptor of the first basic metamorphosis—between the material and the work of art. The twentieth-century sculptor need no longer disguise the fact that works of sculpture are made out of something—on the contrary, it becomes a point of honour not to conceal the fact that the sculpture is also a piece of wood or stone or cast metal or an assemblage of iron bars. Out of this transmutation comes part of the magic of modern sculpture.

In another section of *The Sculptor's Aims*, Moore emphasizes the importance of 'Observation of Natural Objects' : 'The human figure is what interests me most deeply, but I have found principles of form and rhythm from the study of natural objects such as pebbles, rocks, bones, trees, plants etc.' Moore is here chiefly concerned with enriching the *formal* qualities of his work, but as he later says : 'Abstract qualities of design are essential to the value of a work, but to me of equal importance is the psychological human element. If both abstract and human elements are welded together in a work, it must have a fuller, deeper meaning.' To see how this is done—and it has been done with consummate success—we must look at the works themselves.

Moore's subject matter is comparatively restricted; his sculptural interests have always been concentrated, and it is from this that his strength derives. By far the largest single group of his sculptures are those of the female reclining figure—this is the theme that is central to his work. The horizontal figure has certain purely sculptural advantages: for example, it is much easier to support than a standing figure, and does not need to rest on two legs. This may sound obvious, but once a degree of freedom from naturalistic forms is permitted, the supporting legs do pose a particular problem for the sculptor. The reclining figure is much less restrictive, and allows an altogether richer formal vocabulary.

Moore was very quick to appreciate this. Around 1930 he was working on two series—one of reclining figures, the other of standing figures, often holding a child. The latter were more often than not half length, cut off at the waist, so the difficulty with the legs was avoided. He has continued both sculptural series, but the reclining figures are justly the more famous today.

The reclining figure had other advantages for Moore. It was perhaps a less explicitly maternal image than the mother and child, but this encouraged him to look for other ways of giving some sort of timeless, elemental quality to his sculpture. For without needing to go far in the direction of psychological explanations, it is evident that Moore is obsessed by this mother image. It is not an obsession on a personal plane, but on a universal one. Though obviously he must draw upon his own experiences, they are sublimated into a conception that is greater than self. And the fact that Moore has won a far more widespread acclaim than any other sculptor of our age arises precisely because—sometimes without knowing exactly why—people all over the world can see that his sculpture has a quality that is relevant to themselves.

For I take it that Moore's sculpture is essentially a humanist statement of faith, strongly tinged with a kind of Wordsworthian pantheism. He has sometimes made sculptures of specifically Christian subject matter—the *Madonna and Child* for Northampton, for example—but in the last resort these are not entirely convincing. They are done with reverence and humility, but without belief; and one senses an inhibition and a hesitancy in the works themselves. The Northampton Madonna lacks the power and genuine monumentality of the *Reclining Mother and Child*, where no such doubts can be discerned.

The *Reclining Mother and Child* is a late work, made in 1960–1. The female figure is reduced to a strange bony structure that seems
92

Henry Moore *Reclining Mother and Child* 1960–1
(bronze, 86″ L)

somehow to contain two great hollows, one of them empty, the other sheltering the compact form of the child. There is no trace of naturalism as such in the work, and yet the intimate and tender relationship between mother and child is made quite explicit. The larger form is clearly protectively cradling the smaller one. The fact that the work is considerably more 'abstract' than the Northampton Madonna in no way diminishes its human feeling: on the contrary it seems to me to enhance it.

The reason for this conclusion—which may be surprising to some—is simply the *layers* of meaning that the later work, unlike the earlier, possesses. And here we return to the theme of metamorphosis, but in a more subtle and ambiguous form. For Moore's sculpture has an immensely *suggestive* power, on both conscious and unconscious levels, that has arisen from his whole way of working.

Henry Moore *Reclining Woman* 1930
(green Hornton stone, 37″ L)
National Gallery of Canada, Ottawa

Henry Moore *Reclining Figure* 1939
(elmwood, 81″ L)
Collection Gordon Onslow-Ford, California

This is most easily displayed by going back to look at some of his earliest works. Take the Hornton stone *Reclining Woman* in the National Gallery of Canada, for example. Here the figure is like some great expansive landscape, the breasts and legs hillocks and rolling hills. The rhythms of landscape formation are incorporated into the sculpture, together with the rhythms of the body, and this, together with the hard stoniness of the carving, makes us feel at once that here is some kind of earth goddess, existing outside our time and yet expecting our homage.

Henry Moore *Two Piece Reclining Figure Number II* 1960
(bronze, 102″ L)

The analogy between figure and landscape is confirmed in later works, particularly when the sculptor starts to carve great cave-like apertures into the figures. Moore has admitted to being fascinated by caves in hillsides and cliffs, and these holes open up the forms in a remarkable way. Concavities now become as important as convexities, and this is something that had never before happened in sculpture, tied as it always has been to the essentially convex forms of the human figure. But once you are inside the sculpture, so to speak, all sorts of new formal and rhythmic possibilities are implied. As Moore has said: 'A hole can have as much shape-meaning as a solid form.'

This feeling of 'getting inside the sculpture' fitted exactly with Moore's intentions. The sensation of being enclosed, as in a cave, gives rise to a whole series of associations, both prehistoric (for man's first shelters were in caves) and pre-natal (for the cave is analogous to the womb). And it is such associations that underlie the Humanism of Moore's sculptures, emphasizing as they do the antiquity and the continuity of existence, and our particular link, through the mother, with this chain of birth and rebirth.

Henry Moore *Two Piece Reclining Figure Number II* 1960 (bronze, 102″ L)

It is also significant that Moore's figures are more bone than
flesh. It is the durable core of the body that chiefly interests him,
the part that survives the longest, lying in the earth or fossilized
into stone. Erotic and sensual qualities are hardly apparent in his
work, but this does not mean that the figures lack vitality—far
from it. Who can look at the pregnant *Seated Woman* of 1957, for
example, without feeling that it is pulsating with an inner life?

Henry Moore *Seated Woman* 1957
(bronze, 57″ H)
detail opposite

Henry Moore *Upright Motives Numbers 7, 2 and 1: Glenkiln Cross* 1956
(bronze, 126" H)

Henry Moore *Upright Motive Number 8* 1956 ▶
(bronze, 78" H)

On pages 104/105
Henry Moore *Two Piece Reclining Figure Number 1* 1959
(bronze, 76" L)

In all these sculptures of women there are enough references outside the human to remind one that we are a part of the larger world of nature. The study of organic growth in plants and animals as well as in ourselves, has helped directly to shape the sculptural form. This has been so important for Moore that he has on occasions left out the figure altogether. Nowhere is this clearer than in the *Upright Motives* of 1955–6. There are body references in them, but the figure does not give the overall shape to the sculptural form. Instead we have something that is more like a totemic image, a fetish for the twentieth century.

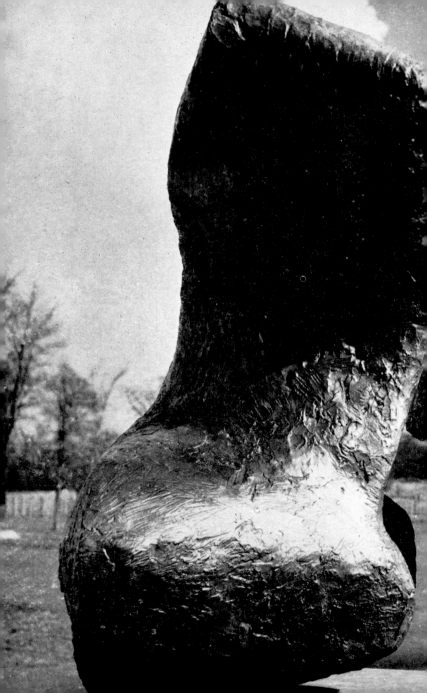

Henry Moore *Upright Motive Number 1: Glenkiln Cross* 1956
(bronze, 132″ H)
Collection W. J. Keswick, Glenkiln, Dumfries

Henry Moore *Upright Motive Number 1: Glenkiln Cross* 1956
(detail) (bronze, 132″ H) ▶
Collection W. J. Keswick, Glenkiln, Dumfries

The *Glenkiln Cross* is a case in point. It stands in a bleak moorland setting, in the kind of unspoiled nature that Moore considers the proper surroundings for his work. It looks at first like a Christian cross, but closer inspection proves this to be untrue. We cannot exactly describe what we see: the stump of a limb, the knob of a bone, some scratched inscription or hieroglyph, all seem to contribute to this over life-size towering image that speaks more to unconscious levels of our experience than it does to reason.

Jacques Lipchitz *Figure* 1926–30
(bronze, 84″ H)
Courtesy of Marlborough-Gerson Gallery, New York

Such totemic images are not uncommon in twentieth-century sculpture. We find them in Barbara Hepworth, whose *Icons* and *Menhirs* have a spirituality that only a classical purity of form can give. Two other artists whose work has already been discussed have also produced remarkable examples—Lipchitz and Brancusi. Lipchitz worked on his over-life size *Figure* for several years before exhibiting it in 1930; it marks a striking development in his work, away from the early cubist sculpture towards a more surrealist imagery. There is a deliberate appeal to unconscious responses here; the forms retain the logical clarity of cubist figures, but they have lost their figurative reference and are now so precisely articulated as to become unreal. Picasso's fear that Cubism, if taken to the abstract, would turn into decoration, is almost realized—the lower part of the *Figure* is like a decorated column carved by some primitive tribe. And yet it is surmounted by what we can only regard as a baleful head, transfixing us with a piercing regard. Lipchitz has made a terrifying piece of sorcery.

Brancusi's *Spirit of Buddha* has some of the same qualities; again we are strongly reminded of a primitive idol. There seems to be no very explicit African or Oceanic influence in Brancusi's work, but the feeling of an object created by a culture less sophisticated than our own is unmistakable. The columnar structure is equally plain, and the figure reference equally oblique but strong. There is no imitation of body forms, but we see a head and a neck the moment we look at the sculpture. The eyes are wide pits in a regular oval shape, they seem blind rather than seeing, and the whole sculpture becomes what Brancusi's title suggests—an earthly repository for the spirit of the god.

As we have already seen, sculpture was for Brancusi a means of meditation to a spiritual end. He knew that there were different ways of striving towards his goal, and what is perhaps most noticeable is the degree to which the shapes he carved and the final form of the sculpture are dependent on the material he was handling. A block of stone would lead him to one solution; a trunk of wood to another. And this is the subject of the next chapter.

Constantin Brancusi *The Spirit of Buddha* (*Kings of Kings*) 1937
(wood, 118⅛″ H)
Collection The Solomon R. Guggenheim Museum, New York

Auguste Rodin *Eternal Spring c.* 1900
(marble, 30″ H)
Hermitage Museum, Leningrad

4 The exploration of materials

A hundred years ago every work of sculpture was made of either bronze or stone; there were no real alternatives to these two materials. Today the situation could hardly be more different. Though bronze retains its primacy, we now accept that sculpture can be made out of anything—it is simply an art form that exists in three dimensions, and lacks the useful character of architecture. Sculptors have been free to try every sort of material. They have felt a new awareness of the qualities of the traditional media; and the exploration of the materials of the modern age has resulted in sculpture being given new forms and new meaning. This has revolutionized the art.

Looking back, one is astonished at the limitations that Rodin would have experienced as a young sculptor. Of the two traditional approaches, modelling and carving, the latter had almost completely disappeared. Wood or stone carving was considered to be the work of a labourer, or at best a craftsman—certainly not something that an artist would do. He modelled in clay, using his hands and working through his fingers. But his occupation remained a more physical one than that of the poet or painter or composer, and perhaps for that reason was socially less acceptable. The manual labour that sculpture involves often causes suspicion.

Granted this physical involvement, however, sculptors seemed to do their best to minimize it, and the making of the final product of their art was literally out of their hands. Clay is impermanent and, even if baked hard (as a terracotta is) it remains delicate and unsuitable for anything except a small work. So the clay is translated into another material by complicated mechanical processes that are almost always undertaken by specialist craftsmen, and not by the sculptor himself. If the clay model is to be cast in bronze a plaster cast is usually made first, and then used for the bronze impressions. Several of these are produced, all equally good.

One should not belittle the qualities of bronze. It is a noble material, and the medium of much of the greatest sculpture from the Greek to our own times. It has maximum durability, so that, once made, it will remain more or less unchanged for ever. It is almost indestructible—a great deal more of the sculpture of the past would survive were bronze not also so valuable and expensive a metal. It has always attracted vandals intent on melting down works of art for the sake of the raw material out of which they are made.

The sculptor may not handle the material directly, but while he works in clay or in plaster he knows what the final bronze will look like. He knows what is possible with such a metal, and what kind of surface texture can be reproduced. He knows, too, that the surface will be coloured with a patina, though to some extent the end result here is a matter of chance.

The sensibility with which a great sculptor today handles bronze is in striking contrast to the sort of thing that happened a hundred years ago. Then, because casting is a mechanical process, any number of casts of a popular sculpture would be made, sometimes rather carelessly and without the supervision of the sculptor himself—perhaps even after his death. In such circumstances the borderline between original work of art and reproduction becomes dangerously blurred.

Nowhere was this more clear than in the case of nineteenth-century stone sculpture. As has been said already, this was not carved by the artist himself, as Michelangelo or Donatello or the masters of the Chartres portals had done. The sculptor produced a clay or plaster model, and with the use of a pointing machine—a simple structure for measuring exactly all dimensions of a three-dimensional object—this was reproduced in stone. Highly skilled craftsmen saw to this: once the model was provided the sculptor himself did nothing at all. Also, working from the model, it was just as easy to make the stone sculpture (or the bronze for that matter) exactly half the size or twice the size of the original, or whatever dimensions were required. Small wonder that most nineteenth-century stone sculpture looks totally dead to us today: the mechanically finished surface effectively stifled whatever spark of creative imagination there may once have been.

One of the most far-reaching innovations of modern sculpture has been the revival of direct carving. For it was obvious to the young men at the beginning of this century that a stone sculpture was not necessarily such a lifeless object. As in so many other respects, Rodin had pointed a way: even though he did not carve himself, he watched his craftsmen very closely, and would make them leave certain areas rough-cut. With Rodin comes the break with the all-over smooth surface that was expected from a marble sculpture.

Paul Gauguin *Idol with Pearl* 1895–8
(bronze, $9\frac{1}{2}$″ H)
Marlborough Fine Art Ltd, London

Even more significant for Brancusi and Epstein and Modigliani and the others in Paris in those tremendously exciting years before 1914, was the revelation of archaic and primitive sculpture. Slowly the Western artistic consciousness pushed the frontiers back, and became aware of the sculpture of more remote ages and civilizations. This is a process equally clear in the history of painting, and here Gauguin's name must be mentioned as the man who more than anyone else suggested new and broader horizons for art.

Gauguin enjoyed the physical part of the artist's activities and would turn his hands to anything. He was a very remarkable sculptor, both as a modeller—he preferred the ceramic medium, making pots of extraordinarily free forms—and as a carver. He liked carving wood in the manner of the primitive peoples whose lives he preferred to share rather than accept the values and demands of so-called advanced Western society. He opened the eyes of younger artists to the artistic qualities of things that had hitherto not been regarded as art at all.

Encouraged by the examples provided by Rodin and Gauguin, and inspired by the wonderful carvings of the distant past or of remote communities, Brancusi and other sculptors of his generation turned back to wood and stone. Brancusi had been a carpenter before taking up sculpture, so he had already imbued the craftsman's approach, but for others the use of chisel and hammer was something that had to be slowly learned. But it was immensely rewarding, as still younger sculptors like Henry Moore and Barbara Hepworth were to find.

It is important to emphasize again the essential difference between the true carver's art and that of the modeller. It is quite another kind of sculpture. The carver is not building up a form with his fingers, but cutting it away with the help of his tools—as Michelangelo says, he releases the image that he can envisage imprisoned in the block of stone or wood. He needs to be immensely sensitive to his material, and immensely skilful in his handling of it.

Paul Gauguin *Huia* 1895–8
(bronze, $14\frac{1}{8}''$ H)
Marlborough Fine Art Ltd, London

117

Henry Moore *Head of Time/Life Draped Reclining Figure* 1953
(bronze, 11″ H)
Collection The Artist

Modern sculptors have realized that the material dictates the
forms of their sculpture. We have already seen how Henry Moore
named 'Truth to Material' as the first of the sculptor's aims and
noted his insistence on preserving the hard, concentrated quality
of stone right through to the finished work. Different kinds of stone
also make different demands, this is something that Barbara
Hepworth in particular has explored. Unlike Moore, she has remained primarily a carver, although since 1950 she has frequently
worked in bronze and has also used sheet metal and other more
experimental media. But her stone and wood carvings are unique.
The material, whether translucent white alabaster or black slate,
has helped to shape the form itself : the form in turn seems to hold
some essence of the material. One is caught at a still centre of
creation.

In a similar fashion, the wood carvings of both Moore and
Hepworth express something peculiar to the nature of this most
gentle of all materials. Wood offers the sculptor a restricted shape
to work from, but the tall slim form of the tree suggests the same
aspiration and striving towards the heavens that the Gothic
cathedral embodies. Wood is an organic material too : something
that has grown, leaving the traces year by year in the pattern of
graining. As he works it, the sculptor can feel this ; the hard knots
hold him back and establish the nodal centres of the sculpture's
rhythmic structure.

Henry Moore *Reclining Figure* 1959–64
(elmwood, 90" L)
Collection The Artist

Barbara Hepworth *Figure* (*Nyanga*) 1960
(elmwood, 36″ H)
Collection The Artist

So far we have talked about a new feeling for old materials, including some, like wood, that had been scorned by sculptors for centuries. What is perhaps even more striking about modern sculpture is the introduction of materials, both old and new, that had never been used for sculpture before.

This new development begins in a spectacular fashion with the Italian futurist Umberto Boccioni (1882–1916), who published in Paris in April 1912 *The Technical Manifesto of Futurist Sculpture*. What is perhaps most extraordinary about this is that, when he wrote it, Boccioni seems to have done no sculpture whatsoever. He immediately set to work, however, to put his principles into practice, and a year later he exhibited his sculpture, first in Paris, then in Rome and Florence. The public was outraged : Boccioni had achieved his purpose. He stopped making sculpture altogether, and returned to painting.

Thus Boccioni belongs among the painters who have contributed so much to modern sculpture. He saw a certain opening, filled it and then retired, just as Picasso was to do. He knew Picasso's cubist head of 1909 (p. 31), but he went further in the analysis of the planes of a head or a bottle, extending them into the space around. He learned from his compatriot, Medardo Rosso (1858–1928), who had tried to find sculptural expression for the almost intangible forms of the Impressionists—evoking a conversation in the garden or the smile on a woman's face or fleeting figures seen in a street at night. Rosso had striven for the sculptural impossible, crushed too by the greater genius of his contemporary Rodin, whose figure of *Balzac* (p. 17) owes something to the Italian. He was still alive when Boccioni hailed him as the precursor of modern sculpture, but he had long since stopped work.

Boccioni was particularly interested in the way that Rosso's figures merged with their surroundings. He referred to him as the only great sculptor who had tried to 'render plastically the effect of environment and atmospheric ties that bind it to the subject'.

Medardo Rosso *Man Reading* 1892
(bronze, 10″ H)
Collection, The Museum of Modern Art, New York

Umberto Boccioni *Bottle in Space* 1913
(bronze, 24″ L)
Collection Mr and Mrs Harry Lewis Winston, Birmingham, Michigan

Medardo Rosso *Small Laughing Woman* 1890
(wax over plaster, 8¾″ H)
National Gallery of Modern Art, Rome

Medardo Rosso *Lady with a Veil* 1893
(wax over plaster, 27″ H)
National Gallery of Modern Art, Rome

The extensions of an object into the space around it was the central doctrine of the futurist aesthetic, which Boccioni himself did much to evolve and propagate. In both paintings and sculptures of 1912, for example, he takes as his subject his mother seated on a balcony overlooking the street. The light and sound and movement of the street below enter through the window, penetrating the solid form of the woman seated in her chair. 'We will break open the figure, and enclose it in its environment,' Boccioni demanded.

In the sculpture, the resulting image is a strange one. The titles — *Head+House+Light*, or *Fusion of a Head and a Window* — give us a clear indication of what is going on. Boccioni is original (or naïve) enough to attempt an almost literal interpretation—he models his mother's head in plaster, but the forms that cut into it are represented by parts of actual glass windows and wooden frames embedded into the plaster.

Most of Boccioni's sculptures survive only as poor photographs, and they were not perhaps particularly beautiful works of art. Their importance lies in the incorporation of materials that nobody previously had conceived could possibly be utilized in sculpture. In his *Manifesto of Futurist Sculpture* Boccioni went even further. He said that sculptors ought to work with 'twenty different materials—glass, wood, cardboard, iron, cement, horsehair, leather, cloth, mirrors, electric light, etc.'

In this extraordinary proclamation Boccioni gave a programme that is still being implemented. He did not in fact take it very far himself, turning instead to another basic preoccupation of the Futurists, the representation of movement. His masterpiece is the *Unique Forms of Continuity in Space* (1913), a figure striding forward, in the sculptural succession of Rodin's *St John* (p. 14) and *The Victory of Samothrace* (which the Futurists compared unfavourably to a racing car). But this was made in plaster, and cast in the conventional and traditional material of bronze, and despite its marvellously rhythmic quality and its spiralling dynamism, it represents a moment of caution on Boccioni's part. Perhaps he very wisely wanted to make sure of its survival.

Umberto Boccioni *Unique Forms of Continuity in Space* 1913 (bronze, $48\frac{1}{2}''$ H)
Collection Mr and Mrs Harry Lewis Winston, Birmingham, Michigan

Boccioni's idea of using twenty different materials for sculpture
accords exactly with the most advanced development in contemporary painting. For in 1912 Picasso and Braque had reached
a formidable dilemma: they had taken cubist analysis so far, and
their pictorial reconstructions were now so elaborate, that the
figure or still life they were painting had become almost totally
unrecognizable. This was the so-called 'hermetic' phase of Cubism.
They had either to give up the pretence of working from something
seen, and construct their pictures out of the abstract elements they
had evolved to represent a figure or still life; or they had to find
some new link with the real world and introduce it into their
pictures. In fact they chose the latter course, leaving Mondrian
and Malĕvich to take Cubism into the new art of abstraction or
non-figuration. Braque and Picasso made contact with reality by
introducing it literally into their pictures, in the form of collage
and *papier collé*—using a matchbox lid or a cut-out piece of
newspaper stuck on to the paper or canvas to represent the
matchbox or the newspaper in the still life group.

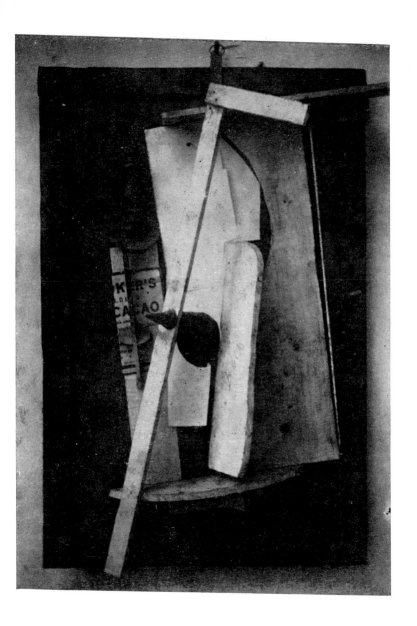

Pablo Picasso *Absinthe Glass* 1914
(painted bronze, with silver spoon, $8\frac{1}{2}''$ H)
Collection, The Museum of Modern Art, New York

This 'invention' had an immediate sculptural application, and Picasso did in fact experiment with three-dimensional collages made out of wood and paper. In 1914 he made the *Absinthe Glass* which incorporates a glass, modelled in plaster with a side cut away, with a real spoon and a lump of sugar resting on top of it— the whole object subsequently cast into bronze and painted bright colours. Although he returned to similar ideas much later in his career, Picasso never repeated the *Absinthe Glass:* it was a demonstration of a certain possibility that, once made, did not need to be made again.

Almost immediately following the introduction of new materials, two distinct types of new sculpture make their appearance. The difference is a simple one—either the material is a means to an abstract end, or it preserves certain intrinsic associations that the sculptor willingly exploits. One could give these two tendencies the labels of the rival *avant gardes* of the twenties and thirties— Abstract and Surrealist. And one can further distinguish them by pointing out that each tendency leads into something that is no longer sculpture or painting, though intimately related to each, the *construction* and the *assemblage*—two art forms that did not exist before the twentieth century.

The abstract-constructivist direction was established by two
Russians, the brothers Naum (born 1890) and Antoine Pevsner
(1884–1962), the former better known by the name he took to
distinguish himself from his brother, Naum Gabo. There can be no
doubt that the younger brother was the more original and inventive.
As a child he was precociously gifted in many fields, and his early
studies were in philosophy and engineering. When he turned
decisively to sculpture in his early twenties, he analysed the situation
as a scientist might, and decided that what was needed was an art
that would express the new ideas of space and time current in
contemporary scientific and philosophic thought. 'Naum was
anxiously looking for new paths and forms in painting, sculpture
and architecture,' another brother wrote. 'He maintained even
then that neither Cubism nor Futurism would be the style of the
future, but what the style would be, he still did not know.'

Naum Gabo *Constructed Head Number 2* 1916
(sheet iron, 17$\frac{3}{4}$" H)
Collection The Artist

Gabo experimented by constructing heads out of wood and sheet metal which made no use of a skin or outer surface. The space occupied by the head was defined by flat planes running across and through it. The result was a sort of blue-print for a head without mass or volume—ingenious, but as long as he remained tied to the image of man Gabo could not get much further. The revelation came when Gabo returned to Russia in April 1917, just after the February Revolution. The atmosphere was a most stimulating one that encouraged every kind of artistic experiment. The leading revolutionaries were Malĕvich, one of the first to paint completely abstract pictures, and Tatlin (1885–*c*.1956), who was making abstract constructions out of metal and wood which owed more than a little to the collages of the Cubists.

Head 1916

Gabo must certainly have found Tatlin's work and his ideas very stimulating. His whole background had made him the artist-engineer whom Tatlin envisaged as the man of the future who would bring art to the new revolutionary society. At all events, Gabo's ideas crystallized, and in 1920 he published what he called *The Realistic Manifesto*, and produced the first of an entirely new kind of art work which he called a construction.

The Realistic Manifesto—it is now usually known as *The Constructivist Manifesto*—is short, clear and to the point. It was written by Gabo to explain his opposition to Tatlin and his followers, who were now taking the view that art was dead, and that the artist must turn to practical tasks in the service of the Revolution. Gabo denied this, and affirmed instead that the future needed an entirely new art form—an art that rejected modelling and volume and mass in sculpture, in favour of space and movement. This led him to make sculptures that owed more to the Eiffel Tower and the Crystal Palace than to Michelangelo or Rodin.

140

The construction as conceived by Gabo is a classical art-form, abstract in content, allowing no place for autobiography or association. It has a strong architectural quality, which helps it escape the yardstick of human scale that we almost inevitably apply to sculpture. It is rational and logical, concerned with balance, proportion, rhythm, movement—this implied rather than actual, though later developments have incorporated kinetic effects. From the beginning, Gabo chose materials hitherto unused by sculptors or, better still, the new inventions of a scientific age. He needed transparent materials to avoid the impression of mass—this meant at first using glass in a metal framework, but later plastic sheet and wire provided Gabo with everything he needed. He has retained the ideal of a new art serving society at large; and the feeling of light and air and movement in his work has a positive, forward-looking quality.

Gabo and his brother left Russia in 1922. Pevsner eventually settled in Paris, and in the latter part of his life executed his constructions in metal, usually bronze, to give them the solidity and permanence that plastic materials did not possess. Gabo remained more faithful to his first principles; he lived in Germany, then in England from 1935 to 1946; and today in the United States. His influence has not been widespread, but it has been profound.
142

The use that the Constructivists were making of metal and plastics encouraged others to experiment. The American, Alexander Calder (born 1898), cut simple shapes out of sheet metal and hung them on wire, which he then suspended from above. In such a way in 1931 the 'mobile' was born, and movement, so strongly implied in work as different as that of Boccioni and Gabo, came into sculpture. Calder certainly added a note of gaiety and good humour, but the very arbitrariness of the many positions the mobile must pass through has proved a serious limitation to any further development of moving sculpture.

Alexander Calder *Spinning Top, Curly Bottom* 1963 (iron, 90″ H)

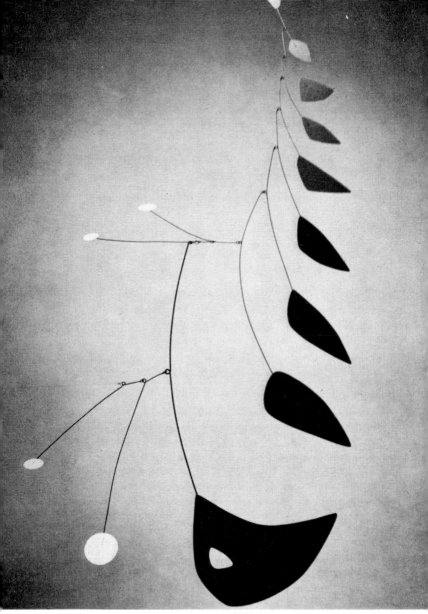

Alexander Calder *Four White Dots* 1959
(iron construction, 56" H)
Perls Galleries, New York

Pablo Picasso *Construction* 1930
(iron, 88″ H)
Collection The Artist

Of much greater significance has been the widespread use of metal, and especially iron as a sculptural medium. This really begins with the group of works that Picasso made between 1929 and 1934. He was helped by an old friend and fellow Spaniard Julio Gonzalez (1876–1942), who had been trained as a goldsmith and began experimenting with iron sculpture in 1927. Gonzalez's own sculptural inventions were at first conventional, and it was not until Picasso saw the formal possibilities of this new medium that his own work suddenly blossomed. Picasso seized on a kind of open-work construction with which Lipchitz had in fact been experimenting several years before. His iron sculptures are sometimes like drawings in space, constructed entirely out of wire, bent and twisted to suggest volume, yet remaining as transparent as a Gabo. Sometimes sheets of metal are introduced, to define a plane in a more forcible manner; and sometimes actual objects are incorporated into the metal structure.

Jacques Lipchitz *Circus Scene* 1927
(bronze, 14″ H)

This brings us to the second, surrealist-assemblage tendency that was mentioned earlier. For Picasso's sculptures are invariably figurative—the iron frame suggests a figure or a head and Picasso confirms and elaborates upon the suggestion, instead of suppressing it. The found object is taken up, isolated, and becomes something quite other than itself—this is the metamorphosis discussed in the last chapter and both Picasso and Gonzalez are masters of it.

What concerns us here is this introduction into sculpture of a new medium—iron—and the exploration of its sculptural properties. In the later 1940s a whole generation of younger sculptors took up this most intractable of materials, and the use of oxyacetylene equipment became as much a part of the sculptor's trade as the use of a chisel had been in the twenties and thirties. Working with iron did not necessarily mean a figurative image. Reg Butler (born 1913) for example, in the early phase of his career bent iron into the shapes of men and women, but he also made cage and tower constructions, like the one that won him the Unknown Political Prisoner competition in 1953. Nor does iron sculpture restrict the sculptor's formal language. The metal can be used in sheets, in ribs and in rods, not to mention the possibilities open if one is prepared to incorporate ready made or 'junk' objects. The difficulty in handling the material, that was once found so discouraging, has now disappeared: carving and modelling are now the difficult ways of making sculpture. Iron can be torn and burnished to give an extraordinary range of effects, but there would seem to be a fundamental bias against volume, and an emphasis on structure. It is this hard, clear-cut quality that is very evident in the work of David Smith (1906–65) and Anthony Caro (born 1924), and their work stands out among the hundreds of sculptors using iron. More than human dimensions give it a dignity and a monumentality and a lack of ponderousness that belie the rather uningratiating quality of the raw material.

Reg Butler *Final Maquette for Unknown Political Prisoner Monument* 1952
(bronze wire on plaster base 18˝ H)
Academy of Fine Art. Berlin

David Smith *Cubi I* 1963
(stainless steel, 124″ H)
Collection The Artist

David Smith *Voltri XVIII* 1962
(iron, 40″ H)
Courtesy of Marlborough-Gerson Gallery, New York

This exploration of materials continues. The most notable characteristic of the work of the youngest generation of British sculptors is that iron is in its turn giving way to new plastic materials which can be shaped with comparative ease. They can also be coloured, and this has resulted in an entirely new range of sculptural possibilities that are now being investigated. The images are sometimes bold and brash, but they have the exuberance and confidence and general lack of gloomy introspection that is typical of the work of this generation. There is certainly no evidence that the vitality has gone out of sculpture. On the contrary, in England at least, much of the best artistic talent is to be found among the sculptors. The regeneration of the art begun by Rodin still proceeds, and the stimulus provided by new materials and new attitudes to old ones goes far to explain why this should be.

Anthony Caro *Sculpture II* 1962
(steel painted green, 142″ L)
Kasmin Gallery, London

Acknowledgments

The Author and Publishers would like to express their thanks to the following who supplied photographs. (References are to page numbers.) Where no separate acknowledgment is made the photographs were provided by the owners of the works.

Arts Council of Great Britain 60
Irving Blomstrann 137
Brassaï 87, 88, 147
Chevojan, Paris 85
A. C. Cooper Ltd 86
Courtauld Institute of Art 29, 65, 81, 133
Walter Drayer 75
David Farrell 76
Galerie Maeght, Paris 45, left 144
Giacomelli Venezia 47
Hanover Gallery, London 42, 43, 81
Joseph Klima 130
Kim Lim 155
Marlborough Fine Art Ltd 4, 6, 34, 58, 67, 152, 153
Marlborough-Gerson Gallery, New York 138
Morgan-Wells 2
Roland Browse and Delbanco, London 15
Service de Documentation Photographique 59
Slawny 36
Sotheby and Co. 30
Studio St Ives 71, 72, 73, 74, 121, 123
Marc Vaux 32, 149

So far as possible, the ownership of a sculpture is mentioned in the caption. This is not always done in the case of works in bronze where several identical copies exist, unless the owner has supplied the photograph.

Some Books about modern sculpture

General books

Sculpture: Theme and Variations by E. H. Ramsden
Lund, Humphries and Co. Ltd, London 1953

Sculpture of the Twentieth Century by Andrew C. Ritchie
Museum of Modern Art, New York 1953

The Art of Sculpture by Herbert Read, the Mellon Lectures of 1954
Faber and Faber Ltd, London and Bollingen Series, New York 1956

La sculpture de ce siècle by Michel Seuphor
Griffon Neuchâtel 1959

Contemporary Sculpture: an Evolution in Volume and Space by
Carola Giedion-Welcker
Faber and Faber Ltd, London and George Wittenborn Inc., New
York 1961 (revised edition)

A Dictionary of Modern Sculpture edited by Robert Maillard
Methuen and Co. Ltd, London 1962

Modern Sculpture. Origins and Evolution by Jean Selz
George Braziller Inc., New York 1963

A Concise History of Modern Sculpture by Herbert Read
Thames and Hudson Ltd, London 1964

Monographs

Art by Rodin
several editions, including Peter Owen, London 1958

The Sculptures of Picasso by Daniel Henry Kahnweiler
Rodney Phillips, London 1949

Gabo with essays by Herbert Read and Leslie Martin
Lund, Humphries and Co. Ltd, London 1957

Henry Moore: Sculpture and Drawings, introduction by Herbert
Read
Volume I 1921–1948 edited by David Sylvester
Lund, Humphries and Co. Ltd, London, revised edition 1957
Volume II 1949–1954 edited by Alan Bowness
Lund, Humphries and Co. Ltd, London, revised edition 1965
Volume III 1955–1964 edited by Alan Bowness
Lund, Humphries and Co. Ltd, London 1965

Jean Arp by James Thrall Soby
Museum of Modern Art, New York 1958

Brancusi by Carola Giedion-Welcker
George Braziller Inc., New York 1959

Barbara Hepworth by J. P. Hodin
Lund, Humphries and Co. Ltd, London 1961

Henry Moore by Will Grohmann
Thames and Hudson Ltd, London 1960

Lipchitz by A. M. Hammacher
Thames and Hudson Ltd, London 1961

Marini by Edouard Trier
Thames and Hudson Ltd London 1961

Rodin by Albert Elsen
Museum of Modern Art New York 1963

Brancusi by Ionel Jianou
Adam Books. London 1963

Medardo Rosso by Marguerite Scolari Barr
Museum of Modern Art, New York 1964

Giacometti by Peter Selz
Museum of Modern Art, New York 1965

There are also several series of useful small monographs on modern artists, among them

Artists of Our Time
Bodensee-Verlag, Amriswil, with an English text
(Armitage, César, Chadwick, Manzù, Penalba, Zadkine, etc.)

Art in Progress edited by Jasia Reichardt
Methuen and Co. Ltd, London
(Armitage, Max Bill, Chadwick, Hepworth, Paolozzi, etc.)

Modern Sculptors edited by A. M. Hammacher
A. Zwemmer Ltd, London
(Arp, Chadwick, Gonzales, Hepworth, Laurens, Lipchitz, Marini, Moore, Picasso, Richier, Zadkine, etc.)

List of Sculptors and Illustrations